Matching

PHOTOGRAPHY

George Siede and Donna Preis

CONSULTANT

Istar Schwager, Ph.D.

Publications
International,
Ltd.

Kate lost a button.
Where can it be?
You'll find that button.
Just look and see!

Tickle, tickle, laugh and giggle.

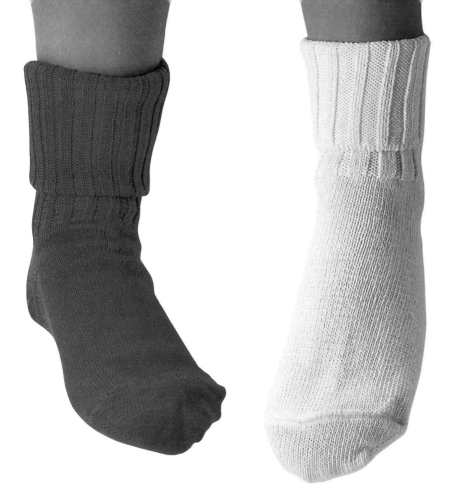

Match the socks as they wiggle.

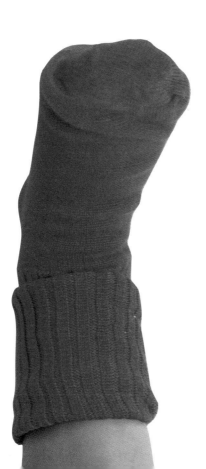

Theodore Thatcher is
A butterfly catcher.
Can you help him become
A butterfly matcher?

Each of these rows is a guessing game.

Matching is what the game is about.

Two things in each row are just the same.

Can you try to point them out?

Four things are all in a row.

But only two things match.

Which are they? Do you know?

Tell me, what's the catch?

What a mess!
What a sight!
Match the pairs,
Left and right.

Here is the cake.
It's missing a piece.
Here is the baker.
Her name is Denise.
One piece is gone.
Where can it be?
Look out for clues.
See what you see.

Which hat goes on whose head?
Who wears blue? Who wears red?

Who wears yellow? Who wears pink?
Who wears black? What do you think?

—— Remember this rule while you play this game: ——

—— Things that match are not always the same. ——

—— Now, what goes together? What are their names? ——

—— Each of these rows is a guessing game, too. ——

—— Which things go together? Do you have a clue? ——

—— Here's a hint—imagine the jobs they do! ——

What goes together?
What makes a pair?
Some pairs you play with.
Some pairs you wear.

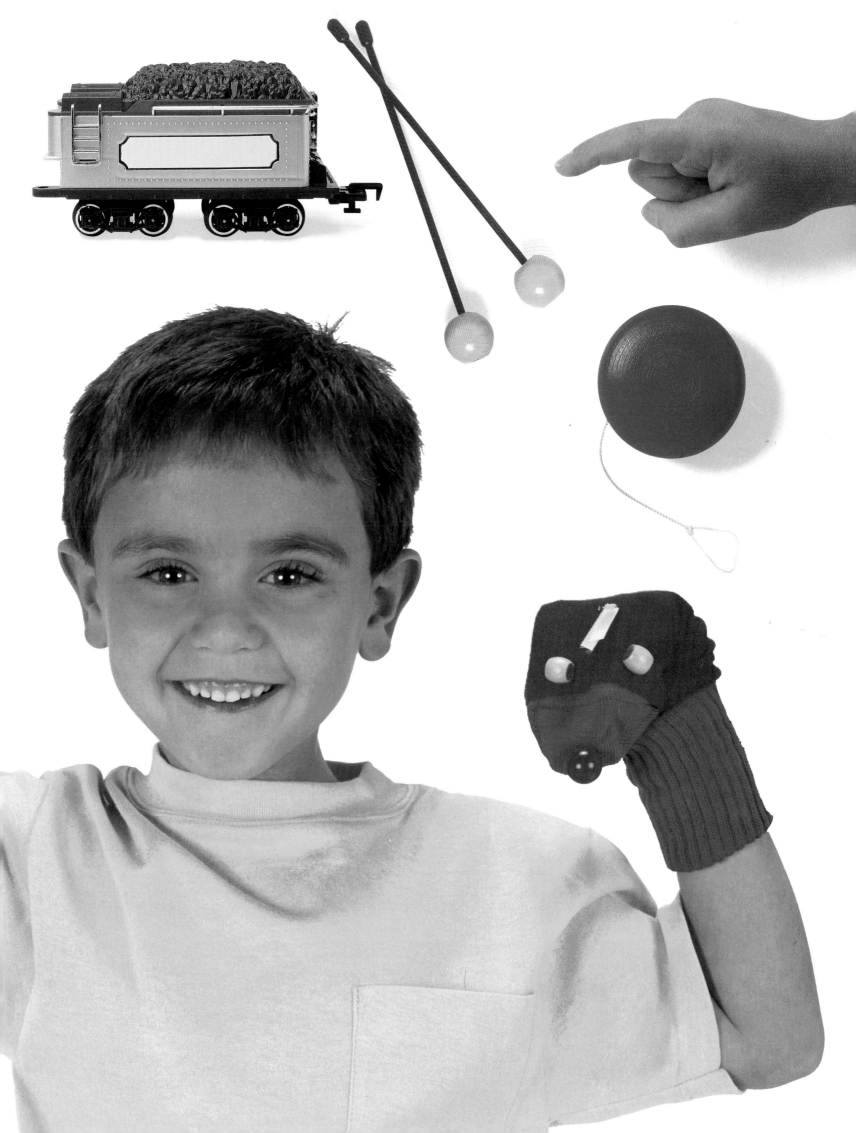

For more fun, take another look

Button, Button

How many buttons can you count?

How many buttons have two holes?

Count all the blue buttons.

Which button do you think is prettiest?

Wiggle and Tickle

How many socks have stripes?

Is one foot different from the others? Why?

Do you have a pair of socks like any in the picture?

Do you like to have your feet tickled?

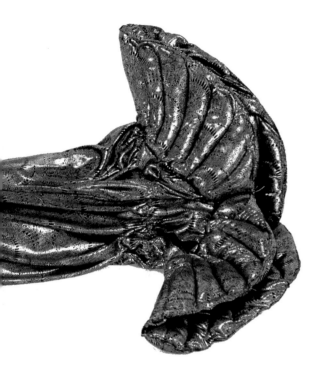

Mixed-up Gloves

Did you find five pairs of gloves?

How many gloves have stripes?

Would you rather wear gloves or mittens?

Think of some other kinds of gloves besides winter gloves.

Piece of Cake!

How many slices of chocolate cake do you see?

What is your favorite kind of cake?

If you were in charge of cutting this cake, how many slices would you cut?

Dress-up Fun

How many children are there?

Who do you think would be the best juggler?

Who would probably ride a horse?

If you could wear any costume, what would it be?